Making CAMPING and OUTDOOR Gear

A Practical Guide to Design & Construction

David Platten

DAVID & CHARLES

Newton Abbot London North Pomfret (vt)

Platten, David
 Making camping and outdoor gear.
 1. Camping – Equipment and supplies
 I. Title
 796'.54'028   GV191.76

 ISBN 0-7153-8023-0

    ISBN 0 7153 8023 0

    © David Platten 1981

Photoset by Northern Phototypesetting Co, Bolton
and printed in Great Britain
by Redwood Burn Limited, Trowbridge & Esher
for David & Charles (Publishers) Limited
Brunel House Newton Abbot Devon

Published in the United States of America
by David & Charles Inc
North Pomfret Vermont 05053 USA

Contents

1 Getting Started

The reasons

Making your own camping gear saves money, since you don't have to pay for anybody else's profit margin, nor for your own labour. Making your own gear allows you to produce the exact variation on the standard article to suit yourself. Making anything can be fun; it's a satisfying way of filling in spare time when you can't spend it out of doors camping.

These are the usual arguments in favour of Do-It-Yourself. First, let me say that I shall not be using that objectionable phrase again; and secondly, that I doubt the arguments themselves. It's not that these assertions aren't true; simply that they aren't complete and therefore can be misleading. Anyway, for me, the real reasons for making my own gear are much more exciting.

To begin with, commercial gear is mass produced. It has to be, if the manufacturer is going to survive in what is now a viciously competitive market. Of course, camping being the way of life that it is, rather than a sport, there is a genuine camaraderie amongst manufacturers: they all have the same enthusiasms, for a start. But underlying it there's a determination on the part of each and every one of them to make you buy his gear rather than someone else's. So the manufacturer invests heavily in research and development to produce the most functional and efficient article possible, to produce a better item than the next man. And having done that, he has to make as many of these articles as possible to recoup his costs.

All this research and development is marvellous. As users of the equipment we benefit enormously, but then as campers we probably all have individual styles and some of the stereotyping of equipment becomes irksome. It's routine and standardisation that we go to the hills to escape, after all. However, the freedom we enjoy is founded on being master of basic routines – like how to pitch a tent in the wet or how to take a compass bearing. Making our own equipment presents a parallel situation, in which individual style is stamped on established method. One of the greatest, if sneakiest, pleasures we can derive from making our own camping gear is to learn and master the findings of the commercial manufacturers' research, so as to produce a satisfying piece of equipment that is not only suited to our particular needs but is based on carefully researched designs that have been well proven in the field and made from the high quality, sophisticated materials developed specially for the manufacturers, at their expense, rather than ours. It's a subtle combination and extension of the three basic arguments.

It's also likely to cause something of an uproar, if only because it's still an oversimplification. Manufacturers make – because they have to – what people are likely to buy, and in any case are usually quite willing to modify their gear for us if asked. As far as costs are concerned, manufacturers buy their materials in bulk direct from the producers, whereas we buy small quantities from a retailer who will have added probably as much as fifty per cent for his own mark-up; and he may well have bought from a wholesaler who has also added a similar profit margin. Our savings can be whittled down to something as low as twenty per cent. You can get more than this in discount from some equipment retailers, through bulk buying. Then there's the satisfaction angle. It's nice to know that every seam in your asymmetric cross-ridge stressed-skin mountain tent was made by you; not so nice to know that you're also responsible for every crooked stitch and wrinkled panel. Few pieces of home-made gear can match the quality of finish apparent in the best commercial equipment, though I've seen some very shoddy commercial workmanship as well.

So where's the advantage in exploiting the manufacturers' expertise? They can meet our requirements, beat us on quality and – if we take our time and effort into account in costing our home-made gear – they charge no more than is reasonable. I believe the advantage lies in the intangible delight of learning by experiment, in gaining understanding and experience of how equipment works. For this, the price of good home-made gear is time and effort and missed television programmes.

6

The work area

The trouble with making anything is that before you can actually start, you have to get yourself organised. You need tools, workspace and time, and all three have to be fitted into your normal daily lifestyle. In making tents and sleeping bags, for example, you're dealing with much larger areas of fabric than when running up a skirt. So you need a large table with plenty of space either side of the sewing machine. For cutting out, you'll probably need the floor, and that could mean moving the furniture about. If the family all have to eat off their laps for a week because the dining room table is covered with Holofil and Ripstop, or you have to wrestle with the sofa every night before you can draw out a pattern, you'll end up trying to manage without doing either and the quality of your work will suffer.

If possible, you want a room specially reserved for the work and containing only the essentials of furniture. Apart from a table and chair, it's helpful to have a small bookcase that will stand against the wall. The shelves will keep the tools you need much more accessibly than a box or work basket. Alternatively, if you're really keen, a sheet of peg board screwed to 20mm × 40mm softwood battens on the wall and a few clips bent up from coat hanger wire will provide the most convenient storage of all.

A good overhead light should be supplemented by a bright and movable table lamp. An Anglepoise is the most efficient answer, and if you can find one that clamps to the table, so much the better. You'll run less risk of knocking it over as you swirl great sheets of infinitely expandable Holofil around the sewing machine.

A small occasional table to one side of your chair provides a useful area on which to place tools that you're using at the time: scissors, tailor's chalk, pins and so on. If you leave these on the main work table you'll spend half your time rummaging for them under your work or picking them up from the floor, onto which you've knocked them.

There are a few further improvements you can make. You can buy vices that clamp to a table top — useful for metalwork. You can set up a separate sturdy work bench for the hammering and sawing part of equipment making, and you could set up a drawing table for design work; but on the whole it's best to keep everything as simple as possible.

In practice, you'll probably have to use the dining room table, the sitting room floor, and relegate the work on hardware to the garage. This doesn't make the work impossible by any means, but it does result in your having either to spend time setting everything out and packing it away every time you want to put in a couple of hours' work, or having to live with the mess. The importance of this factor is often underestimated.

Recycling materials

Since, for the majority of us, circumstances will dictate that we live with our equipment while it's in the making, now is the time to mention the gentle art of opportunism. To benefit most fully from making your own gear, you have to live, eat and sleep with your mind on equipment. Every item of clothing, household junk and piece of furniture takes on a new dimension as you examine it from the point of view as to whether it can be modified for use in the outdoors.

For example: if you take one of the heavy aluminium foil dishes in which monosodium glutamate pies are sold, punch a hole in the centre and screw the burner head of a Primus stove through it before inserting the burner into the fuel tank, you have a heat reflector which can cut boiling time dramatically in the field. Some shampoos and hand creams come in small plastic squeeze bottles with nozzles. After washing out with hot water and bicarbonate of soda and widening the hole, they make handy dispensers of clear jams, honey and washing-up liquid. When bivouacking without a tent in midge-country, I used to sleep with my head inside a fine-mesh nylon shopping bag, through the top hem of which a draw string was threaded. It was quite useful on extended camps for side trips to the local grocery store as well.

The handle of my backpacking spoon has a vee-shaped nick filed in the end, turning it into a two-pronged fork. The waist strap on my climbing sack, complete with quick-release buckle, came from the seat belt of a scrapped motorcar. My candle holders are made from baby's feeding bottle teats with the bulbs cut off. Even my

8

camp slippers are made from the vinyl seat of an old easy chair. With effort and dedication you can build yourself quite a reputation for ingenious improvisation – although your friends might think of different names for it. It's all good harmless fun really.

In theory, you never throw anything away without first considering its potential as a piece of outdoor equipment. In practice, you never throw anything away, ever. Now you see what's meant by having to 'live with the mess'.

Studying the market

Browsing through the equipment stores and the catalogues, the magazine advertisements and the camp sites teaches you much about construction and materials as long as you keep asking yourself, 'Why is it made like that?' Why, for example, is polyurethane-coated nylon made up into garments with the proofing on the inside? The answer is simply that the PU coating is easily damaged by abrasion with rocks and rucksacks, and putting it on the inside helps to protect it. Why does a Sigg fuel bottle stopper have a transverse hole drilled through it at the top of the threaded portion? In fact it allows the pressure to be equalised inside and out on the first half turn, so making it easier to remove. Noting details like these will improve the quality of your own design.

You'll also be able to notice the types of material used for different types of equipment, and form some opinion as to their suitability. Tents used for youth groups tend to feature PVC wavelock material for groundsheets. It's heavy but it's strong and, most importantly, it's easily patched with a scrap of the same fabric and a smear of Bostik No 1. Patching PU-proofed nylon isn't so easy. The glue either strips the proofing off or seems reluctant to stick.

Some makes of down-filled sleeping bags and duvets use brown or grey down inside lightweight, pale-coloured Ripstop nylon. The filling is clearly visible through the fabric and, to my mind, unsightly, so I use slightly heavier fabric in darker colours.

The other main point to watch for is the 'commercial appeal' of any product. The Cyclops Echo rucksack, for example, features a suede-covered base. It's supposed to resist abrasion better than nylon – though the only hole rubbed in the one I used to own was in that suede base – but it absorbs water and attracts mud, however often you spray it with silicon-based sealant. It's real purpose may be implicit in the comment made by one equipment store manager I spoke to: 'You try selling a pack without it.' The same applies to striking, two-tone cagoules and pretty stripes on sleeping bag shells. Neither feature improves performance; it just sells the product, and we don't need to bother with the extra work which such trimmings demand. As always, the rule is to keep it simple.

2 Materials

Nylon

Synthetic fabrics, and in particular nylon, probably account for ninety per cent of the materials from which outdoor gear is made. We shall be touching on metal – specifically aluminium – and on the techniques most suited to amateur metalwork, but generally speaking, amateur gear-making means sewing textiles.

The basic nylon fabrics that we're most likely to use are made from continuous filament fibres spun into yarn and tightly woven into taffetas in a variety of weights ranging from less than $50g/m^2$ to over $500g/m^2$. It's worth noting at this point that most materials these days are sold by metric measure; unfortunately, this is by no means universal, and confusions abound between the price lists of various suppliers. For consistency, I shall be quoting exclusively in metric throughout this book, but the conversion table on page 152 should help to solve any problems.

As an outdoor material, nylon taffeta has tremendous advantages. It is virtually impervious to rot, very strong for its weight, resilient, abrasion-resistant and capable of accepting a bewildering range of finishes and coatings to suit an equally bewildering variety of uses. The acid-dyed colours are fast, bright and, though subject to eventual fading in the ultraviolet element of sunlight, relatively long lasting.

The nylon yarns which form the fabric are smooth and slippery; so, untreated, the weave is liable to open up under stress. To prevent this, the fabric can be calendered – passed between heated rollers which melt the surfaces and partially fuse the yarns to each other – producing the familiar, shiny finish.

Softer materials, easier to work with, more pleasant to wear, and showing some of the more desirable qualities of natural fibres like cotton and wool, can be produced by chopping up the nylon

11

filament and crimping it before spinning it into a yarn. The resultant slightly fuzzy finish is less subject to distortion in the weave than is plain taffeta, breathes more readily and provides better insulation. Anti-Glisa nylon, a lightweight fabric, Taslan, a medium-weight version which is so far only available as a Goretex laminate, and Cordura, a heavyweight looking like canvas and used mainly for rucksacks, are three prominent trade-names.

Another variation on plain taffeta is Ripstop nylon. In this process, extra-strong threads are introduced at intervals as both warp and weft, thus giving the weave its characteristic squared pattern. In theory, the grid of strong threads checks any tendency of the fabric to tear if punctured. It's worth bearing in mind, though, that when coated with a waterproofing PU film it can lose its anti-tear qualities.

Polyester fabric belongs to a rather different family of plastics, but since it features extensively in clothing, sleeping bag inners, and tents, for which nylon is also used, it's most conveniently mentioned here. It bears a marked resemblance to cotton in texture; and, indeed, it is usually blended with the natural fibre to produce a cheaper yet harder-wearing material. It is supposed to be more absorbent than nylon, though I find that it makes me sweat profusely and doesn't mop up the perspiration very well either. It does, however, make good tent inners in light weights, as it sets better than nylon.

Goretex

Both nylon taffeta and polyester fabrics can be purchased laminated with a microporous film of PTFE – the stuff that goes on non-stick saucepans – as Goretex, the registered trade-mark of W. L. Gore & Associates. This material, though costing about twice the price of the basic textiles, is perhaps the most significant recent innovation in outdoor fabrics.

Its virtue is that while being totally waterproof – it will resist water entry pressures in excess of $3.9kg/cm^2$ – the PTFE film sandwiched between the outer fabric and an inner knitted-nylon backing allows water in vapour form to pass freely through it. Shell clothing made from Goretex does not suffer from condensation due

12

to perspiration collecting on the inner surface, so theoretically your inner clothing does not wick the moisture back, and therefore remains dry.

Goretex is not, of course, designed actually to stop you sweating and does need care in maintenance as it is susceptible to contamination from body oils. As a new fabric it is undergoing continuous development and improvement, and after working with it and living in it I am thoroughly convinced by it.

W. L. Gore & Associates actually manufacture the material in $63g/m^2$ and $100g/m^2$ taffeta or Tazlan finishes, in $167g/m^2$ polyester/cotton and in a soft Antron knit, in a wide range of colours. It's also available as a two-layer laminate without the knitted backing – a useful variation for garments being made in double thickness material. A special $63g/m^2$ taffeta variation with an ultra-lightweight backing is available for making single-skin tents. In all versions, the standard roll width is 140cm. You may find some difficulty in obtaining anything other than the taffetas, since it's expensive stuff for suppliers to stock until demand is established; but it only needs to be asked for often enough . . .

Proofings

The only other way to produce a totally waterproof nylon fabric is to coat it with something. The heaviest-duty coating is probably PVC. I like to use $267g/m^2$ PVC-coated nylon taffeta for groundsheets as it provides a finish that is smooth on both sides and therefore picks up mud less readily. PVC Wavelock fabric is even heavier, consisting of a thick film of the plastic in which is embedded a reinforcing mesh of loosely woven nylon rather than being simply a coating applied to a taffeta. PVC can also be used to coat lightweight knitted fabrics, which are usually made up with the knitting on the inside. It's a comfortable material but, the coating being very thin and exposed on the outside, it is to my mind easily damaged.

For medium and heavyweight fabrics used in clothing, neoprene coating probably offers the best compromise between hard wearing and flexibility. Most commonly, it comes in $267g/m^2$ weight, though $134g/m^2$ can sometimes be obtained. It is less subject to damage by abrasion than PU coatings, which have also been known to delaminate with wear, but is less suitable for lightweight applications.

Polyurethane coatings – the PU referred to on earlier occasions – is still the most common, even on heavyweight fabrics. It provides a tough, flexible, waterproof finish and can be applied in various thicknesses depending on the weight of fabric to be proofed. Lightweight nylons are usually obtainable with PU rather than neoprene coatings.

A more recent development for lightweight fabric is a polymeric coating, which bonds better to the nylon and results in a material up to five times stronger than the equivalent weight of PU-coated nylon. This is the fabric for waterproof stuffsacks, re-usable bivvy bags and lightweight tent flys.

Totally waterproof coatings do suffer some problems, the main one being their susceptibility to condensation. Moisture vapour from sweat or, in tents, damp clothing and foul-weather cooking, cannot escape and so collects on the impervious surface. In extreme cases of cold, wet weather – the very conditions in which you most need to keep warm and dry – the inside of a waterproof garment can seem as wet as the outside.

For sleeping bags, therefore, from which moisture must be allowed to escape, for duvets and ultra-lightweight tent inners, a silicon-proofed nylon is better. In this case the fabric is impregnated with a silicon wax which repels water partly by filling the interstices of the weave and partly by reacting with water to alter its surface tension, thus causing it to roll off rather than penetrate. At the same time, it allows moisture vapour to pass through. Unfortunately, it washes out easily and needs reapplying regularly; this is easily done, however, using a proprietary solution like Grainger's Fabsil. The real disadvantage of silicon proofing is that it will never withstand the high water entry pressures associated with heavy rain. In other words, it isn't waterproof.

Whatever system of proofing is used, there are problems with the seams of any nylon garment. The fibres being locked into position either by calendering or proofing, no needlehole will close up once made. With every pass of the needle, therefore, an inlet for water is formed. Goretex is particularly vulnerable in this respect, and some

14

manufacturers have taken to welding the seams of items made in this material, rather than sewing them.

To some extent, the problem can be reduced by using special thread consisting of a polyester or terylene core wrapped in cotton. The core provides the strength while the cotton sheath swells in the damp to fill the needleholes. Then there are particular types of seam which mask the stitching, and which we shall be looking at later. The easiest way to waterproof seams, though, is with a specially formulated sealant. Some of these contain solvents which attack the proofing on the fabric and are therefore not very helpful. Mesowax and Karrimor Seam Seal both work well, though, and are obtainable from good camping shops. Seams in Goretex are best sealed with Seamstuff, marketed by W. L. Gore & Associates and readily available from their Dunfermline plant (address in Appendix 1). Bostik No 1 also works satisfactorily.

Pile fabrics

The easiest material from which to make warmwear is the now familiar fibrepile fabric. It consists of a knitted base, forming the outer surface, with a thick, fluffy backing of tufted filaments air-blown through the fabric to form an insulating layer on the inside. The knitted surface is then treated with resin to inhibit pilling – the forming of little balls of fluff on the surface, which would eventually lead to its breaking down. Pilling used to be a significant problem with this material but recent improvements have gone far towards eliminating it. Some commercial fibrepile garments, like the Javelin Super 'S' range, have a fine knitted nylon bonded to the surface, which improves windproofing and effectively eliminates pilling altogether.

For the amateur gear-maker there is little choice of grades or weights of fibrepile fabric, although several types are available to the commercial manufacturer. Nevertheless, the standard fabrics stocked by the suppliers can be used for clothes, sleeping bag liners, or – so basic it's almost cheeky – a decadently luxurious groundcloth for the inside of your tent. I can vouch for the comfort of this last application, but it's rather too bulky a piece of equipment for backpacking!

Stretch fabrics

Not strictly a pile fabric, but excellent for warm underwear, is lightweight tracksuit or sweatshirt material. This knitted stretch nylon with a brushed finish can be made up into teeshirts and long pants, or into sleeping bag liners less bulky than any made from fibrepile fabric, yet almost as warm. Even better, if you can get it, is thermolactyl fabric of the sort used by Damart for their underwear. They cannot supply fabric to the public – and don't seem too keen on selling their finished products either – but it's occasionally available in market stalls and remnant shops.

In searching for such material, you will probably also come across the prequilted nylon used in popular chainstores anoraks. For specialist outdoor equipment, it's not really worth buying, since it offers much poorer insulation than a good fibrepile fabric.

Helanca is another warm synthetic fabric with a certain amount of stretch built into it, which makes it very suitable for breeches or trousers. With such material, these garments can be made fairly close fitting, yet allowing complete freedom of movement around knees and seat, especially important in the more gymnastic pursuits like rock climbing. Being a synthetic, it does not absorb water very readily, and dries out quickly if it does get wet. The only trouble is that, for as long as it is wet, it's horribly clammy; and it's very difficult to get hold of.

Coming a close second in terms of performance – and readily available from most drapers – is Courtelle. This is made in several grades and weights; the best is thick, warm, stretchy and hard-wearing.

Fillings

For really good synthetic insulation, Holofil is the only serious – and readily available – consideration for amateur gear-making. Made from very fine polyester filaments, crimped and lightly bonded into a mat, it is still much cheaper than down. It offers about fifteen per cent less insulation and loft, weight for weight, but retains most of its insulating properties when wet. It's also somewhat easier to work with.

16

A single layer of 234g/m² is adequate for two-season sleeping bags or duvet jackets, while a double 167g/m² layer should provide enough insulation for year-round valley use. A four-season mountain sleeping bag or duvet would need at least a double layer of 234g/m² Holofil, but this is still a perfectly feasible proposition as regards the final weight and bulk of the item. In fact, I have just finished testing a home-made sleeping bag constructed from two 234g/m² layers of Holofil which I was able to buy prequilted to a nylon taffeta. Making up two bags to fit inside each other was simplicity itself, and the finished article, which weighs less than 2.5kg, kept me almost too warm on Dartmoor with the thermometer registering −8°C.

Other synthetic fillings available to the amateur don't really offer anything more than Holofil, though one is regularly hearing of 'breakthroughs' with regard to which my own instinct is to let someone else do the testing. The terylene wadding obtainable from market stalls and hobby shops is possibly of some use in duvets and insulated waistcoats, but offers nothing like the loft or long-term resilience of Holofil.

Down

Down comes from the innermost layers of birds' plumage and consists of clusters emanating from a single point rather than from a stalk of any length. It has enormous lofting power, expanding in the heat from your body to produce a considerable layer of dead-still air, which is what provides the insulation. It's also very compressible. In its stuffsack, a three-season down sleeping bag will take up little more room than a large sliced loaf. And, with care, it lasts for years.

Although it doesn't like getting wet, good quality duck or goose down is the best and lightest insulation possible. Surprisingly, it's not too difficult to work with, if you have plenty of time and patience, but it is *very* expensive. My own feeling is that, in view of its price, you want to be very sure indeed of your competence in sewing before committing yourself to doing justice to such a luxury.

Having said this, it may well be worth persuading Granny to sleep under a modern – synthetic – continental quilt, so that you can abscond with her old eiderdown. Unfortunately, such quilts are often not filled with eiderdown at all, but with a blend of chopped and curled feathers, which tend to be full of stalks, tired, limp and incredibly dusty. How to extract the stuffing from bed quilts and feed it into the channels of a down-filled article is dealt with in project 10.

Finding a source of down may not be easy. The suppliers listed in Appendix 1 are helpful but do not always have stocks available for purchase by the general public. Furthermore, quality varies considerably within any given range and it helps to be able to inspect what you're buying before paying for it. However, provided that it's clean, and reasonably free from stalks, it will make very little effective difference to the warmth you'll get from it whether it's best northern goose or Chinese duck, pure down or blended with soft curled feather: amateur construction and filling of down articles just isn't that efficient.

Wool

Of all the natural materials used for outdoor clothing, apart from down, wool offers probably the best insulation. It spins into a soft yarn that traps a lot of air, and in its natural oiled form it contains chemicals that react with water actually to generate heat. Wet wool can be even warmer than dry, provided that it's not exposed to a cold wind which will accelerate evaporation of the moisture with a consequent chilling effect. Apart from this, wool has a 37 per cent saturation point, which means that it can absorb over a third of its own weight in water before it even feels damp.

It's the only material really suitable for socks and, unless it irritates your skin, it makes good mittens, hats and underwear. One of its most useful applications, though, is in sweaters. Traditionally, Scandinavian fishermen wore thick brushed-wool sweaters as their outer garments. The long fibres on the surface acted like thatch in shedding the rain.

Beware of yarns which look like wool but aren't. In practice, wool is often blended with a synthetic fibre to increase its resistence to wear and improve its elasticity. This is fine, as long as the blend contains at least 80 per cent wool: less than this and the properties

18

of the natural fibre begin to be lost. Synthetic knitting yarns like Acrilan and Orlon are useful to people who find that wool irritates their skin. These yarns still trap plenty of air in the fibres and absorb perspiration; but they are not, of course, as warm as wool when wet.

Cotton

Cotton is absorbent and can be very closely woven. When the fabric gets wet, the fibres swell and close up even tighter, yet water vapour can find its way through with relative ease. Thus, heavy cotton canvases and duck can be highly water-repellent, yet breathable. Being absorbent, it responds well to waterproofings, which penetrate right into the fibres; whilst untreated cotton worn next to the skin, as a teeshirt for example, will soak up sweat readily.

When it is wet, though, cotton feels cold and clammy, which is why denim jeans are so definitely unsuitable for outdoor activities. Once they're soaked, they're worse than nothing, because they offer no insulation yet hold water which the wind can then evaporate with potentially disastrous refrigerating effects.

Even the most water-repellent cotton, then, has its dangers when used for clothing. Ventile, the ultimate in cotton outdoor material, is much less waterproof – and less breathable – than Goretex. In fact, Ventile resists a water entry pressure of around $140g/cm^2$ as opposed to Goretex's $3,900g/cm^2$ while allowing for a water vapour transmission of less than $5,000g/m^2$ in 24 hours, which is certainly no better, and in fact marginally worse, than Goretex laminate. And so, Goretex now being available with cotton-feel finishes, Ventile would seem to be obsolete, particularly as there's little difference in the price!

In addition, cotton is subject to mildew, rot and, in cheaper grades at any rate, shrinkage.

Leather

Although plastics are threatening to take over here too, nothing has yet become readily available to replace leather as the ideal material for footwear. When treated with waxes, it is virtually waterproof; it

19

breathes, is flexible, traps air in its pores and therefore offers some insulation, and it's highly abrasion-resistant.

Full-grain, unsplit hide is far too thick for amateur gear-makers to contend with; special tools and skills are needed and you will never achieve anything approaching the standard of commercial boot-manufacturers. However, soft, split leather and suede can be sewn on a domestic machine with leatherpoint needles, or, in heavier grades, can be hand sewn by making thread holes with an awl first.

About the only application which can seriously be considered is in making camp slippers, for which you'll find instructions in project 16. Small leather patches, though, can be used to reinforce pole attachment points in tents, and have the advantage over metal eyelets that the leather swells in the wet and closes up the space around the pole spike, so reducing leakage into the tent at this point.

Synthetic, simulated leathers have little more than a cosmetic application to outdoor equipment, though I have made a pair of vinyl moccasins which look smart enough to wear to the pub and which let me make subsequent excursions from my tent during the night while staying dry-shod. The seams of these are not sewn; just butt-jointed and glued with Vinylweld, a proprietary adhesive sold for repairing car upholstery and sports bags.

Foam

Closed-cell foam, of which the best is Karrimat pressure-blown foam with a waterproof cell structure, is useful for padding the shoulder straps, hip belts and the back panels of rucksacks. For greater flexibility, you might consider using two or three layers of the 3mm mat which can be bought by the metre, rather than the 9mm-thick panels.

Open-cell 'sponge' foam also has possibilities in equipment making. For years I used a 45cm × 90cm pad of 5cm-thick sponge foam as a sleeping mat. It was encased in a $67g/m^2$ PU-proofed nylon taffeta with one end sealed by Velcro. It could be rolled up and secured with a couple of webbing straps, took up no more room than a Karrimat, was just as warm and more comfortable. I've now sunk to the decadence of a short, aluminised airbed but a superior variation on my old mat is in use by several members of my youth group and is featured in project 12.

The trouble with open-cell foam is that it does soak up water so it has to be encased in a proofed fabric, and then you meet up with the old problem of condensation. Nevertheless, with ingenuity and perhaps a little daring, you can make interesting equipment from it. How about a duvet waistcoat with no quilting lines – and no cold spots – from 12mm foam? Or even a pair of extreme cold weather underbreeches?

The main advantage of this material, though, is its relative cheapness and its availability from most hardware stores and craft shops.

Cuffing and webbing

Elasticated, knitted nylon cuffing is available from most outdoor-materials suppliers, and makes the finishing of jackets and breeches much neater. One form consists of a seamless tube, a length of which can be folded back on itself to form a double thickness before stitching to the wrists of jacket sleeves. For jacket or trouser waists, a different form is more suitable. The edge to be sewn to the fabric is not elasticated and so, when the cuffing is bought, appears to be gathered. It straightens out as soon as the cuffing is stretched. Installing it can be a little tricky but if it's carefully tacked in place, rather than just pinned, a neat finish can be achieved. This is also a useful way of finishing the lower ends of breeches legs. The elasticity of the cuffing allows much greater freedom of movement around the knees than the traditional fabric band.

Hip belts for rucksacks and shoulder straps for light day packs call for the 50mm nylon webbing that's used for car seat belts. You can buy this off the reel, but why not visit your nearest car breaker's; and while you're scrounging the webbing, why not pick up the buckle as well?

Narrower, 20mm and 12mm webbing will be needed for rucksack lid straps, accessory attachments and so on, as well as for the leggings and the tents featured in this book.

Climbing tape, as used for slings, is the strongest available, but a thinner, less bulky alternative is available from Thos Foulkes or TOR Outdoor Pursuits and is ideal for the tent projects, nos 14 and 15.

Since they are effectively textiles, but don't fit conveniently into any other category, this is the place to mention guy line and quilting mesh.

The first is available as window-blind cord from hardware stores. Buy the 250kg breaking strain weight. It's stronger than you need, but it tangles less easily than the thinner stuff and it's easier on your hands.

When quilting synthetic fillings to a fabric backing, you'll find the job made much easier if you lay over the top of it a layer of very lightweight nylon netting. The cheapest curtain netting will do. It's much less expensive than an extra layer of nylon taffeta and much lighter. Nevertheless, it will hold the fibres in place rather than letting them engulf the sewing machine.

Thread and glue

For putting it all together, of course, you'll need sewing thread. For lighter weight applications, Coates Drima polyester thread, available from haberdashers, is perfectly suitable. For waterproof clothing, rucksacks and tents, I prefer Koban 75 industrial thread with a polyester core and a cotton sheath which expands with wet to fill the needleholes. This comes in 1,000 metre reels; you'll find yourself using it simply to avoid running out all the time. The little 100 metre reels of Drima don't last long!

A little less obvious is glue. Wavelock PVC, for example, can be strongly welded into a totally waterproof seam with Bostik No 1. Vinylweld works excellently on heavier vinyls. Leather and other natural fibres can be secured with Copydex or Evostick. Where appearances don't matter, glue can often be used to produce a temporary join which is reinforced with stitching. Awkwardly positioned seams in heavy fabric, such as in rucksacks, can prove easier to make by this method. If you equip your workshop with a range of glues and adhesives you will avoid the temptation of using an unsuitable glue which may fail under arduous conditions.

Zips and Velcro

Plastic-coil zip fasteners can be bought in any length required. The ends of the zip are not finished in any way and either have to be turned in at right angles to the line of the zip and sewn into the hem to which the zip is attached, or sealed by sewing across the end and reinforcing with glue.

The sliders come separately. Until you get the knack, they can seem impossible to install. The trick is to clamp the slider in a vice, separate the two halves of the zip and feed each one *simultaneously* into the wide end of the slider until the teeth engage at the narrow end. Then pull the slider up to close the zip again.

Open-ended zips, with either moulded or coil teeth and with sliders already fitted, can be bought in a variety of lengths for use with cagoules, jackets and gaiters where you need to separate the two halves of the garment to get into it. Double sliders enable the zip to be opened from both ends at once, to aid ventilation. Extra-long open-ended zips are also available for inserting into sleeping bags.

It's often been said that two simple-quilted bags can be zipped together to form a two-season double for you and your partner, or be used one inside the other for a warm four-season single. What happens to the partner in winter, I'm not sure.

Metal-toothed zips are a thing of the past, which is just as well, since they freeze, corrode, jam, snag the fabric they're attached to and could give you a nasty nip in delicate places if closed in a hurry. Plastic-toothed zips are very much kinder and more reliable, but the lightweight coil zips can be burst open without undue effort and are best avoided for heavy-duty use. For the best in reliability, go for the 9mm moulded tooth zips.

A very useful alternative to the zip fastener is Velcro. This comes as a double tape, one half featuring a host of tiny hooks and the other a fine loop pile. When pressed together, the two halves engage firmly but can be torn apart without difficulty. It's very useful for a multitude of applications, including tent flysheet extensions, map cases, pocket closures, weatherflaps over zips on cagoules, and for trouser flies − where it's much easier to install than a zip. It's available in several widths and colours, can be cut to any length and

23

be machine-sewn directly to the fabric. It will burst open under pressure so is best used where no sudden strain will be applied.

Hardware

In some cases, neither zips nor Velcro are suitable as closures; for example, on the elasticated waistbands that I favour for trousers. (Some people object to these as constricting, but I never find them so and they do make construction a lot easier.) Here, zips are difficult to install, and the hooked portion of a Velcro fastening tends to snag the knitted elasticated nylon cuffing. The problem can be solved with press studs. Small ones, up to about 10mm in diameter, are readily available from haberdashers and should cover most requirements. For really big, heavy-duty applications, try yacht chandlers and tarpaulin manufacturers.

Buttons are another possibility, but as a rule I prefer press studs in any application where buttons might be used, simply because really neat, secure buttonholes are difficult to make in slippery synthetic fabrics, even with a buttonholing facility on your sewing machine. Equally fiddly, and to my mind inefficient in outdoor clothing, are the various other fastenings like hooks and eyes, frogs and toggles. You'll be doing yourself a considerable favour if you design your gear to avoid these.

Eyelets which you can buy in various sizes from hardware stores, complete with punch and die for installing them, are certainly worth considering. Provided that you reinforce the area where eyelets are to go with at least one – preferably two – extra layers of fabric, and cut crosses for them in the fabric rather than punching circular holes, they can provide strong attachment points for tent pegs, neat grommets for the spikes on the tops of tent poles, or convenient lacing holes for compressible packs, stuffsacks and so on.

Some manufacturers prefer to use small aluminium 'O' rings placed over a hole in the fabric and secured by oversewing with several layers of stitching. A development of this idea is the 'D' ring, so called because of its shape. These can be secured to fabric with loops made from strips of the same material or with nylon webbing. The loop passes round the flat side of the 'D' ring and is sewn

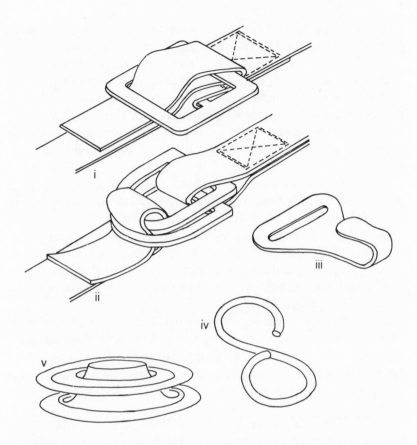

fig 1 Hardware: *i* simple locked buckle, *ii* 'D' ring buckle, *iii* flysheet (or gaiter toe) hook, *iv* 'S' hook, *v* eyelet

strongly into a seam or onto a reinforcing patch. For use with straps up to about 25mm, a couple of 'D' rings sewn together into the end of the webbing make a secure buckle. The strap is passed through both rings together, then back over one and under the next. 'S' hooks are also useful, consisting, as the name implies, of an 'S' shaped hook open at one end and closed at the other. A more sophisticated alternative is the fly-sheet hook, useful as a gaiter toe clip or linkage between tent inners and fly.

For rucksack straps, at the point where the wide, padded shoulder strap is joined to the narrower tension-adjusting tape, proper non-slip buckles are better, if you can find them. As is so